Harry Potter™

MAGICAL CREATURES

A MOVIE SCRAPBOOK

WIZARDING
WORLD

INSIGHT ◉ EDITIONS

San Rafael • Los Angeles • London

CONTENTS

+·+·+·+·+·+·+·+·+·+·+

CREATURES OF HOGWARTS

INTRODUCTION

As seen in the Harry Potter films, the story of Harry's journey, from the day he finds out he's a wizard to his liberation of the wizarding world through his defeat of the Dark Lord Voldemort, could not be told without the creatures he encounters. These creatures provide companionship and help build his character as he navigates through his years at Hogwarts School of Witchcraft and Wizardry.

Harry arrives at Hogwarts with an owl named Hedwig, as first year students are allowed to bring an owl, a cat, or a toad with them. Hedwig becomes a comfort and helper to him. Through the years, his friends also bring creature companions to school: Ron Weasley has a rat; Hermione Granger, a cat; and Neville Longbottom, a toad (though he seems to lose him frequently). The professors and staff at Hogwarts have their own companions as well—from Dumbledore's phoenix, Fawkes, to caretaker Argus Filch's beloved feline, Mrs. Norris.

In addition to wand duels and exams, Harry is challenged through his years at Hogwarts by an assortment of magical creatures, including a proud Hippogriff in his Care of Magical Creatures class, mysterious Thestrals, mischievous Cornish pixies, and the Hungarian Horntail dragon he must defeat in the Triwizard Tournament held in his fourth year of school. All these interactions become opportunities to improve his skills and test his mettle. There's nothing like unexpectedly having to dodge a huge three-headed dog named Fluffy to see if you've got what it takes!

One Hogwarts student, Newt Scamander, who attended the school decades before Harry did, loved the wizarding world's creatures so much he became a Magizoologist to study magical beasts of all shapes and sizes. The film *Fantastic Beasts and Where to Find Them* follows Newt as he writes a guide to help wizards understand why every creature should be valued and protected. Newt's interest in the subject becomes his life's work, through which he makes many furry and feathered friends. During his adventures, Newt must recover a thieving Niffler, locate an invisible Demiguise, and entice a female Erumpent when they escape a case that holds the generous environments he has built for his beasts.

Throughout the filming of the Harry Potter movies, followed by *Fantastic Beasts and Where to Find Them*, teams of concept artists, animatronic engineers, model makers, and digital artists, among many other disciplines, gave every creature a unique personality and a believable naturalism. Whether real or magical, the creatures we meet inside Hogwarts and outside in the wizarding world capture our imagination and inspire us to be protectors of our feathered, furry, and scaly friends.

SCABBERS

Scabbers is Ron Weasley's rat, handed down from his brother Percy. Scabbers debuts in *Harry Potter and the Sorcerer's Stone* with his head in a box of candy after Ron meets Harry on the Hogwarts Express. Both real and animatronic rats were seamlessly composited throughout the films to portray Scabbers; the live rat who filmed the most scenes was named Dex. When the box pops off Scabbers's head after Ron casts a badly written spell, it is Dex who emerges, after a trainer pulled away a wire attached to the box.

TIME TO RUN

On their way back to the castle from Hagrid's hut in *Harry Potter and the Chamber of Secrets*, Scabbers bites Ron and runs away. Actor Rupert Grint (Ron) held Dex while walking up the hill, but when Scabbers "bites" him, an animatronic rat dropped to the ground. Footage of Dex running from the drop point across the grass was inserted digitally after the scene was filmed.

ERROL

Errol is a great gray owl owned by the Weasley family, seen in *Harry Potter and the Chamber of Secrets*, where he brings them their letters from Hogwarts listing their needed books and supplies. Errol is played by Zeus, who was trained to fly with an envelope in his mouth and to hop up after lying on his back for a few moments. Both a stuffie and a digital Errol were used when he crashes into the window, and later, in the Great Hall, for a collision with a bowl of chips.

PIGWIDGEON

It took Pigwidgeon, Ron's very tiny owl, a long time to make his big debut. Originally cast for *Harry Potter and the Goblet of Fire* and photographed for *Harry Potter and the Order of the Phoenix*, Pigwidgeon is finally seen in *Harry Potter and the Half-Blood Prince*, in Ron's room at The Burrow, and later, perched on a chair in the Gryffindor common room. Pigwidgeon is played by Mars, a scops owl, which is one of the smallest species of owls.

COMPANIONS

HEDWIG

When Harry Potter is brought to Diagon Alley by Rubeus Hagrid to buy his supplies for Hogwarts in *Harry Potter and the Sorcerer's Stone*, Hagrid gifts him a beautiful snowy owl for his birthday. Named Hedwig, she becomes a trusted ally and loyal companion to the young wizard.

FAKING IT

Radio-controlled animatronic Hedwigs and fake owls called "stuffies" were used in scenes featuring crashes or tumbles. When Harry Potter and Ron Weasley miss the Hogwarts Express in *Harry Potter and the Chamber of Secrets*, they fly in Ron's father's Ford Anglia car to get to the school. Both a stuffie and an animatronic Hedwig were used to film the turbulent ride. The puppet could turn its head the same way as a real owl and could open its eyes wide in alarm when the car narrowly misses crashing into the train once they catch up to it.

TURN OF THE TAIL

In *Harry Potter and the Prisoner of Azkaban*, Harry, Ron, and Hermione learn from Azkaban escapee Sirius Black that Scabbers is the Animagus form of traitor Peter Pettigrew. For the scene, "The animal department shaved bits of [Dex's] fur off so he would look manky," says Rupert Grint, "but he's really a nice, healthy rat who just had a bit of a makeover!" Grint held Dex at first, then a fake rat was grabbed by actor Gary Oldman (Sirius Black) and dropped onto a decrepit piano. Dex ran over the piano and across the floor, then the fake rat hit the wall and transformed into Pettigrew.

TREVOR

Gryffindor Neville Longbottom brings a pet toad named Trevor with him to Hogwarts—though he frequently loses track of it. In fact, Hermione's first words to Harry and Ron aboard the Hogwarts Express are about the lost toad. Trevor is played in the films by a quartet of toads that were held in large, heated moss-based aquariums. Actor Matthew Lewis remembers there was one particular toad named Harry that just didn't like being held and kept trying to jump out of Lewis's hands and onto his face!

CROOKSHANKS

Hermione Granger brings a huge cat named Crookshanks to Hogwarts in *Harry Potter and the Prisoner of Azkaban*. Crookshanks is played by a handful of red Persians. Prince was the best at being carried. Pumpkin caused problems for the sound department as she sometimes purred loudly during filming. Crackerjack was the most versatile and had the most time onscreen.

CAT RACE

Crookshanks literally races onto the screen chasing Ron's rat, Scabbers, at the Leaky Cauldron. It took several months to train Crackerjack and Dex, who played Scabbers, to sprint down a corridor. The rat was supposed to run "in fear" ahead of the cat, but Crackerjack and Dex had become such good friends that they kept running together. So, the trainers would give Dex a head start before releasing Crackerjack after him.

CAT GOT YOUR EAR?

In *Harry Potter and the Half-Blood Prince*, Harry, Hermione, and the Weasley kids' plans to use an Extendable Ear to eavesdrop on the Order of the Phoenix are ruined by Crookshanks, who takes it for a toy. The cats all learned to play with the Ear, then grab it and walk away. After dropping it in a bowl off-screen, they'd be rewarded with a kitty treat.

MRS. NORRIS

Mrs. Norris is a close companion and willing accomplice to caretaker Argus Filch as he looks for students who have broken rules. Four Maine coon cats with different skills played Mrs. Norris. Pebbles excelled at walking down corridors and stopping on a mark. Max could jump and land on actor David Bradley's (Filch's) head or shoulders, and Cornelius was trained to sit in place. Alanis loved nestling in Bradley's arms and was known to fall asleep between filming scenes.

CLICK INTO PLACE

Each cat was trained using a unique system: When the cat pressed a bar on a food bowl, the bar would click and dispense a kitty treat, so the cats associated the sound of a clicker with a reward. Clickers were then used to teach the behaviors needed for a scene. To have Mrs. Norris follow or stand next to Filch, a remote-controlled clicker was installed in Bradley's boot!

FANG

Before casting Rubeus Hagrid's gigantic dog, Fang, the filmmakers auditioned a sizable variety of dogs, including deerhounds and Great Danes. But it was one of the largest and oldest of breeds that got the part: the Neapolitan mastiff. Nine "Neos" played Fang, all rescue dogs, and though intimidating in size, this breed has an extremely gentle nature—and an extremely juicy drool!

SLOBBER SWAP

In *Harry Potter and the Chamber of Secrets*, Harry and Ron enter the Forbidden Forest to speak with the Acromantula, Aragog, accompanied by Fang. Surrounded by Aragog's myriad descendants, they're rescued by the Weasleys' Ford Anglia car. The smallest Neo, Bella, handled the action, though the car still needed an extra-wide back seat for her. An animatronic Fang was used whenever the car moved. The radio-controlled Fang could turn his head and spray out drool, just like the real one.

FLUFFY

When Harry, Ron, and Hermione are discovered in the forbidden third-floor corridor in *Harry Potter and the Sorcerer's Stone*, they hide behind a door, then realize they aren't alone. At first, the students see the head of a sleeping dog. Then there's a yawning second head and a third head that's not too happy about being awakened. As if a three-headed dog wasn't enough, when Fluffy—yes, Fluffy—stands, he turns out to be twelve feet tall!

THREE HEADS ARE BETTER THAN ONE

The digital effects crew felt that each of Fluffy's heads should have its own personality. The head on the far left is the leader and thinks before he acts. The head on the far right is the most aggressive: act first, think later. Fluffy's middle head is a bit dim—it takes him a bit to catch up on what is happening around him.

◆·◆·◆·◆·◆·◆·◆·◆·◆·◆·◆·◆·◆·◆·◆

WOOF, YAP, AND YOWL

To create the sound of Fluffy's growls and snarls, supervising sound editor Eddy Joseph recorded several dogs, including his own. Then he added in a few other sound elements, including the sound of his assistant gnashing his teeth.

FAWKES, THE PHOENIX

Harry Potter is sent to Headmaster Albus Dumbledore's office in *Harry Potter and the Chamber of Secrets*, where he notices a dreadful-looking bird that suddenly catches fire! This is Fawkes, Dumbledore's phoenix. Phoenixes have infinite life cycles: After a long adulthood, they erupt into flames in old age and are then reborn from the ashes.

SENIOR MOMENT

The aged Fawkes has an extended vulture-like neck, missing feathers, and the color of a burned-out match. Though his feathers are scruffy and faded, there are still embers of brightness around his eyes. This version of Fawkes could slide on his perch, react to other characters, and flap his wings. A combination of practical fire effects and digital flames were used when he burst into flames.

FOUR FAWKES

Three animatronic versions of Fawkes were created by the creature shop, for the filmmakers felt it important the actors have something to interact with physically: one at the end of his life and then the reborn chick, both seen in Dumbledore's office, plus a mature adult that helps Harry Potter when he gets trapped in the Chamber of Secrets. Fawkes is a digital creation when he flies. The digital artists observed and filmed real birds for his wingspan, including a blue macaw and a turkey vulture.

◆·◆·◆·◆·◆·◆·◆·◆·◆·◆·◆·◆·◆·◆·◆·◆

WELL HEALED

Though Harry defeats the deadly Basilisk in the Chamber of Secrets, he injures himself on the serpent's poisonous fangs. Fawkes flies in and stands beside Harry. Lowering his head, Fawkes sheds tears onto Harry's wound—for a phoenix's tears have the ability to heal. This animatronic version of Fawkes was the most complex version, which could extend and fold its wings, raise its crest, cock its head, and blink, and it had ducts in its eyes that could actually release liquid tears.

BABY FAWKES

The fledgling Fawkes that emerges from the pile of ashes also has an elongated neck layered with folds and wrinkles. The chick is covered in soft, fluffy gray feathers, with a distinctive crest of pink feathers topping his head.

DEFENSE AGAINST THE DARK ARTS

CORNISH PIXIES

In *Harry Potter and the Chamber of Secrets*, the new Defense Against the Dark Arts professor, Gilderoy Lockhart, uncovers a cage of Cornish pixies for his first lesson, at the same time revealing his questionable abilities. When released, these exasperating creatures pull students' hair and knock books off shelves in a practical effect using thin wires.

TRUE BLUE

The creature shop created a life-size electric-blue model of a pixie for the computer artists to "cyberscan," in which they transform a 3-D object into a digital code. This Cornish pixie was then turned into more than twenty that cause mayhem in the classroom. To give a sense of depth as they dip and dart, pixies were placed in the foreground, middle, and background.

RETURN TO FORM

The Cornish pixies are seen again in *Harry Potter and the Deathly Hallows – Part 2*. When Harry climbs a mountain of furniture in the Room of Requirement to retrieve the Ravenclaw diadem, he unintentionally grabs a pixie and discovers the flock has taken up residence in a mountain of couches and chairs.

VERA VERTO

Professor Minerva McGonagall's Transfiguration lesson in *Harry Potter and the Chamber of Secrets* covers how to transform an animal into a water goblet, so each student has a small creature just waiting to be transfigured, including chameleons, toads, owls, and armadillos. The classroom is also filled with cages holding ring-tailed lemurs, hornbills, and various other mammals that were not to be part of the Transfiguration lesson.

MCGONAGALL'S ANIMAGUS CAT

An Animagus is a witch or wizard who has the ability to transform themselves at will into an animal. Professor McGonagall is one, able to transfigure herself into a cat. McGonagall's Animagus, seen in *Harry Potter and the Sorcerer's Stone*, was played by a tabby cat named Mrs. P. Head, who already had markings around her eyes that resembled the professor's spectacles.

CARE OF MAGICAL CREATURES

HIPPOGRIFF

Groundskeeper Rubeus Hagrid becomes the professor for Care of Magical Creatures in *Harry Potter and the Prisoner of Azkaban*. His first lesson introduces his students to Buckbeak, a Hippogriff, which is half horse, half eagle. The Hippogriff is one of the few composite creatures in the Harry Potter films that allowed for a divide between its two species.

LEAPS AHEAD

When Harry mounts Buckbeak for a flight, Hagrid slaps the Hippogriff's rump and he rears up. One animatronic Buckbeak was designed to perform this action for the film, but when it came to shooting the scene, the amount of time it would take to set and reset the creature for each take would not have been cost effective, so the digital Hippogriff's flight sequence begins with him standing on his back legs before running to take off.

OPPOSITES ATTRACT

Birds have light, buoyant bones, and horses' bones are heavy; each animal's body is structured for different movements. Mixing the two to create a believable Hippogriff wasn't easy. Inspiring the design was director Alfonso Cuarón's idea that Buckbeak might be clumsier on the ground, but when he flew, it was with grace and controlled power.

✦·✦·✦·✦·✦·✦·✦·✦·✦·✦·✦·✦·✦·✦·✦

TWO BY FOUR

Four versions of Buckbeak were created: Three identical life-size animatronic versions—two standing and one sitting—were built by the creature shop, covered in real feathers and simulated horsehair, and cyberscanned for the computer artists. The two standing models could move their wings, nostrils, eyes, tongue, and neck. One of these could curl its claws and splay its wings via aquatronics (water-filled cables), as well as move its right foreleg and left hind leg. The animatronic Buckbeak that sits, condemned, in the pumpkin patch behind Hagrid's hut, used aquatronics and was mounted onto a track so it could be wheeled under shelter at night and in inclement weather. This was the only practical version of Buckbeak seen on-screen. A digital Buckbeak did all the walking, running, and flying.

ACROMANTULA

Harry and Ron start to track down the Heir of Slytherin in *Harry Potter and the Chamber of Secrets* by visiting the Forbidden Forest, looking for an ancient Acromantula named Aragog.

A TRULY GIANT SPIDER

Creature effects supervisor Nick Dudman rejected the idea of a digital Aragog, confident his team could build an Acromantula that climbs out of his hole and speaks with the two young wizards. The spider they created topped two stories, had an eighteen-foot leg span, and weighed two and a half tons.

FOUR BY FOUR

Aragog's movements were a combination of animatronics and puppetry. His front four legs were radio-controlled, using a water-based system for the creature's hydraulics, which could reproduce the creepy gait of a spider. Once the forelegs cleared the hollow, Aragog's back four legs were lifted via a counterweight by a team of puppeteers. The puppeteers only had to push Aragog and he would crawl up out of the hole.

A PART TO PLAY

Aragog's lifelike actions completely unnerved actor Rupert Grint, who has a fear of spiders. Grint asserts that he didn't have to act too much during their scenes together because he was genuinely scared. Daniel Radcliffe also admits that his first glimpse of Aragog was terrifying. The last member of their trio—Hagrid's dog, Fang—was unfazed. In fact, Bella, the Neapolitan mastiff playing Fang for those scenes, took the giant prop to be a toy and caused a bit of damage trying to play with it!

✦✦✦✦✦✦✦✦✦✦✦✦✦✦✦✦✦✦

WEIGH IN

It is a grief-stricken Hagrid who must bury Aragog when he passes away in *Harry Potter and the Half-Blood Prince.* Now shrunken and curled up with age, Aragog was completely rebuilt for the film. To produce the translucent quality of a dead spider, he was made from polyurethane. Though he was lighter in appearance, Aragog still had to slide into his grave the way something heavy would move. For this iteration, his steel skeleton and completely solid body weighed three-quarters of a ton.

THESTRAL

In *Harry Potter and the Order of the Phoenix*, Harry comes upon his first Thestral, a black winged creature that can only be seen by those who have witnessed death. At Hogwarts, Thestrals are used to pull carts that take the students up to the castle. Though they look intimidating, they are quite gentle and regal.

BABY THESTRAL

For the scene in which Luna Lovegood feeds a baby Thestral in the forest, the designers realized its head would not reach the ground, due to its long legs and short neck. So, they looked to real-life animals. Though the closest parallel had a long neck and short legs, it worked: They had the baby Thestral spread its legs like a giraffe, which allowed it to lower its head.

◆·◆·◆·◆·◆·◆·◆·◆·◆·◆·◆·◆·◆

HOLDING SWAY

When Bill Weasley and Fleur Delacour are about to ride a Thestral in *Harry Potter and the Deathly Hallows – Part 1*, the actors were filmed atop horses to get the "swaying" effect of a four-legged creature. Once they took flight, horses were swapped for digital Thestrals. But this posed the question—where did the Thestrals' legs go? The visual artists felt it would look silly if they were "prancing," so the Thestrals tucked their legs in underneath themselves.

CENTAUR

Centaurs are another example of a composite creature, this time, human and horse. In *Harry Potter and the Sorcerer's Stone*, Harry meets a centaur who saves him from an attack by Voldemort. The centaur, Firenze, was a completely digital creation, shadowed under the dark forest canopy.

X
JEWELRY AND
WEAPONRY FOR
THE CENTAURS
WAS HANDCRAFTED
BY THE PROP
DEPARTMENT.
X

CREATURES' FEATURES

Harry Potter and the Order of the Phoenix affords a closer look at centaurs when Harry, Hermione, and Professor Umbridge confront a dozen of these creatures in the daytime. These centaurs have strong equine features: long faces, wide foreheads, eyes set far apart, and flattened noses, jaws, and cheeks. The coloration and fur of their pelts cover their bodies from head to hoof.

DRAGONS

NORBERT, THE NORWEGIAN RIDGEBACK

In *Harry Potter and the Sorcerer's Stone*, Harry, Ron, and Hermione visit Hagrid's hut just as a dragon egg Hagrid has been tending to is about to hatch. (Hagrid always wanted a dragon.) The practical prop egg shakes and wobbles upon a table as they all wait for its occupant to emerge. Air jets blown underneath the table gave the egg its rocking motion.

DRAGON BREATH

For hatching, the prop egg was replaced by a digital version, which breaks open with an explosion of green gas. Then a slimy, drooling, gawky baby Norwegian Ridgeback bursts out. Hagrid names the adorable dragon "Norbert." The computer artists gave Norbert iridescent skin and leathery bat wings but only a hint of a ridge on his back, reasoning this feature wouldn't be developed on him just yet. When Hagrid tickles him under the chin, Norbert sneezes out his first flame, scorching Hagrid's beard. Fortunately, the fire was digital.

UKRAINIAN IRONBELLY

In the darkest depths of Gringotts Wizarding Bank, a giant Ukrainian Ironbelly dragon guards the ancient treasure vaults where Harry, Ron, and Hermione must retrieve one of Voldemort's Horcruxes in *Harry Potter and the Deathly Hallows – Part 2*. Tortured by its goblin keepers, the emaciated Ironbelly has veins popping through its pale white skin, blending with old wounds from mistreatment and rusty chains. Though the dragon is dangerous, it's also terrified, for the filmmakers wanted to evoke sympathy. Reference material of rescue dogs and circus bears was studied to create convincing behaviors for the Ironbelly.

FLIGHT, NOT FIGHT

Once the trio recovers the Horcrux, Hermione forms a mad idea to use the Ironbelly to escape. A life-size section of its back was sculpted and painted, then mounted onto a motion control base for the actors to "ride." The dragon's flight was already programmed in the computer, and this data was exported to the rig, synchronizing movements. Large flying birds, such as an albatross, were referenced for its clumsy takeoff, but once it's airborne, the Ironbelly gains strength and majesty as it flies.

[a]n ancient competition between three wizarding [schools i]n *Harry Potter and the Goblet of Fire*, composed [of ... I]n [th]e first task, each school's champion must wrest a [golden egg tha]t guards it. To select the dragon they'll face, each [champion ...] and pulls out a miniature version of the creature.

TRI WI ZARD TRA GE DIES

TRIWIZARD TRAGEDIES

32ⁿᵈ Edition

[COMMON WELSH] GREEN

[m]agic cham-
[... co]mmon
[... a]rtists
[... draw]ings would
[... fou]nd, which
[...] append-
[...] four legs.

CHINESE FIREBALL

Durmstrang Institute's Viktor Krum draws the Chinese Fireball, whose design evokes the legendary dragons of Asian mythology. The Fireball's coloration of blazing reds and golds pays tribute to Chinese culture.

SWEDISH SHORT-SNOUT

Hogwarts has two champions: Harry Potter and Cedric Diggory. Cedric chooses the Swedish Short-Snout, whose coloration matches his Hufflepuff house crest. Details of scale shapes and snout profiles were explored—the Short-Snout offered easy guidance for the concept artists.

HUNGARIAN HORNTAIL

Harry's dragon is the Hungarian Horntail, which obviously needed to have sharp horns and a dangerous tail. Ideas encompassed a tail with one long spike, rows of spikes, or a cluster of spikes at its tip. The final decision was to have spikes cover the dragon from the top of its head to the tip of its tail.

One of the credits for *Goblet of Fire* reads, "No dragons were harmed in the making of this movie."

A LARGE TASK

The creature shop crafted a full-scale, fully painted version of the Horntail's head and neck for the digital artists to cyberscan. This came in handy when the producers wanted a life-size dragon for Hagrid to show Harry the night before the first task. The Horntail's head was rebuilt in fiberglass to install a flamethrower that shot forty-foot-long fireballs. Then the team fashioned a forty-foot-long, seven-foot-tall dragon puppet, operated by hidden crew members, with a wingspan of seventy feet. Almost three hundred individually hand-painted spikes in six different sizes were placed on the dragon's head and body.

For the second task of the Triwizard Tournament in *Harry Potter and the Goblet of Fire*, the champions have one hour to recover someone dear to them who has been charmed and then submerged in the murky waters of the Black Lake. The task is not easy, especially when the creatures who live beneath the surface impede the champions' goal.

MERPEOPLE

As Harry swims within the lake, he encounters Merpeople, who monitor the task. He rescues Ron as he's supposed to, but Fleur Delacour's sister has not been retrieved, and time is running out. Harry is told by a merperson he can rescue only one of them. The filmmakers wanted creatures with natural, believable anatomies, so instead of being half person–half fish, the merpeople have characteristics of both, with scaly skin, large fishlike eyes, and an upturned mouth filled with pointy teeth.

NEITHER FISH NOR FLESH

The concept artists referenced sturgeons and tuna for the merpeople's extra-long bodies and broke with convention by having their tails move from side to side, rather than up and down.

Early designs suggested octopus tentacles for hair; this was changed to translucent anemone-like strands. To emphasize the merpeople's intimidating nature, traditional lighter coloration for their skin, such as silvers and aquas, was discarded for a darker palette of muddy browns and greens.

GRINDYLOWS

As Harry swims to the surface with Ron and Gabrielle Delacour, he is attacked by Grindylows, impish creatures described as a cross between a nasty child and an octopus. Their final design was based on what the Grindylows needed to do physically: grab Harry and keep him underwater. Two stuntmen pulled on Daniel Radcliffe's (Harry's) legs in a green-screened water tank to mimic the Grindylows' attack.

A FISH-EATING GRIN

The Grindylows became all head and multiple arms, with very little in between except a wide mouth that shows multiple rows of sharp teeth when they grin. More than a hundred Grindylows appeared on-screen, their movement hand-animated with the help of a new software developed by the digital team.

UNDER THE CASTLE

BASILISK

In *Harry Potter and the Chamber of Secrets,* Harry fights the Basilisk, a giant serpent with a deadly stare. As Harry, Ron, and Professor Lockhart make their way into the Chamber, they find the cast-off skin of a very large snake, a preview of the living creature Harry will encounter. The creature shop produced a forty-foot-long prop snakeskin, with the assumption that the living Basilisk would be a digital creation.

GETTING AHEAD

Knowing that when their battle reaches a climax, Harry stabs the Basilisk with the Sword of Gryffindor, director Chris Columbus asked the creature team to make a physical prop of the Basilisk's mouth for Daniel Radcliffe to fight and react to. The team went a bit further, creating a Basilisk head with a functional jaw, a twitching nose, and fangs that could retract for the mouth to close. Then, as the full-size snakeskin had already been produced, they decided to go all the way and craft a practical Basilisk.

CONCEPT ART FOR THE BASILISK INCLUDED DETAILED STUDIES OF THE SERPENT'S EYES.

SNAKES AND LADDERS

The first twenty feet of the Basilisk were created to attach to the animatronic head, with a foam rubber skin and an interior structure shaped by cut-up aluminum ladders. These would keep the creature's body light in weight as it pursues Harry around the Chamber. The Basilisk's body movements were created by aquatronics, giving it a gliding fluidity. A counterweighted pole arm could raise or lower the creature, which was also mounted on a track that allowed it to slide closer and closer to Harry as they fought.

SERPENT SOUND

What does a Basilisk sound like? The Basilisk hisses and roars, and after Harry defeats it, groans in pain. Sound designer Randy Thom put together a mash-up of animal sounds, including horse and elephant vocalizations, a tiger's roar, and even his own voice!

UNEXPECTED VISITORS

DOBBY, THE HOUSE-ELF

House-elves do one master's bidding their whole lives, unless they are given an item of clothing, which frees them. Dobby is a house-elf with big eyes, big ears, and big intentions to keep Harry safe when he shows up at Hogwarts in *Harry Potter and the Chamber of Secrets*, but his "help" often backfires, with Harry getting in trouble or worse. Dobby was originally planned to be a puppet that would interact with the actors before it was decided that he would be the first entirely digital major character in the Harry Potter films.

LOOKING TO THE PAST

To determine Dobby's look, the concept artists considered what his life has been like before he meets Harry. It is clear Dobby has been mistreated, so they thought of him like a prisoner of war. He was given leathery, grayish skin covered in grime and no muscle tone. The animators also thought about his movement: Dobby is often hunched over, and he wraps his arms around himself or curls inward in fear. After Dobby is freed, he stands much straighter.

HEALTHY, HAPPY, AND FREE

Dobby is freed by Harry at the end of *Chamber of Secrets*, and the next time we see him, in *Harry Potter and the Deathly Hallows – Part 1*, he looks much happier and healthier. To illustrate this, his face and neck were smoothed out and his skin was given a soft, rosy glow. His eyes, which had been as big as saucers, were reshaped. Even his clothing has changed for the better—the ratty tea towel he used to wear has been replaced by a clean and pressed towel—and he's wearing a pair of red sneakers!

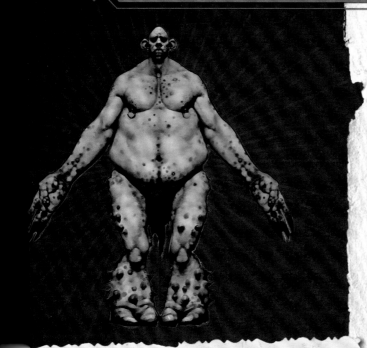

During Halloween in *Harry Potter and the Sorcerer's Stone*, a mountain troll invades Hogwarts and strolls into the girls' bathroom where Hermione is hiding after being teased by Ron. Trolls are not very nice, but they're not very smart either. With a precise "swish and flick," Ron is able to levitate the troll's club, knocking him out when the spell wears off.

NO SMALL PARTS

Several practical versions of the troll were created to help the young actors perform the scene. The troll's hands and legs were generated at full size for Emma Watson (Hermione) to act against as she ran under exploding sinks and toppling doors. When the troll is knocked unconscious and falls on the floor, it's a life-size, costumed clay version. This troll had an animatronic head and fingers that twitched to scare the students into thinking he was coming to.

A FACE YOU COULDN'T LOVE

The troll gave concept artists an opportunity to explore something really ugly—not in the sense of evil, though the troll is aggressive, but for how unsightly a creature could appear. He's covered in thorny warts and blemishes, he has saggy green skin, and yellow teeth protrude from his mouth in several different directions. He also has scraggly tufts of hair in his armpits, on the top of his head, and over his floppy belly.

DEMENTORS

Dementors drain every person in their vicinity of joy and leave them with their worst memories. These eyeless, black-shrouded creatures occupy Hogwarts in *Harry Potter and the Prisoner of Azkaban*, looking for the escaped titular prisoner. The digital designers researched the rotting wrappings of embalmed bodies for their look.

ON HAND

Dementors physically attack Harry in the Muggle world in *Harry Potter and the Order of the Phoenix*. For an even more menacing appearance, their robes were opened, exposing decaying rib cages, emaciated arms, and hands with long, bony fingers. One hand restrains Harry against an underpass wall. Actor Daniel Radcliffe was raised by a rig, but instead of using a practical hand, the digital artist created an effect that simulated Harry's neck being squeezed.

ab067

BOWTRUCKLES

Newt Scamander first became enamored of Bowtruckles while at Hogwarts. They are small, woody creatures, at most eight inches tall, that resemble stick insects and saplings, and nest in wand-quality wood trees. A branch (family) of Bowtruckles live in their own environment within Newt Scamander's case. This branch consists of Titus, Finn, Poppy, Marlow, Tom, and Pickett, who is deeply shy.

OUT OF THE WOODS

Pickett is a bit of a social outcast, much like Newt, and feels bullied by his branch, so he prefers to hide out in the breast pocket of Newt's coat. (While working in his case of beast environments, Newt explains to Jacob Kowalski that Pickett has attachment issues.) Bowtruckles can open locks, which makes Pickett very handy to have around!

FEEL THE REAL

Pickett was a computer-generated creature, but to help Eddie Redmayne (Newt) and other actors, a finger and a rod puppet were used to help them understand what it felt like for a Bowtruckle to walk or stand on their bodies. Puppeteers used the expressive limbs of Pickett's body to create shapes that would indicate whether he was feeling sad, worried, or proud.

SPECIAL FEED CODES

🦜	Beaked (excl. Griffin)		🦅
🪶	Feathered		🦭
🦌	Horned		🐗
	Hooved (not Nogtails)		🦅
🐚	Carapaced		🦗

HABITAT & TERRAIN CODES

	Aquatic / Amphibious		🦐
△	Burrowing		🦡
	Desert		🐍
	Tropical/Equatorial		
	Temperate		

FANTASTIC BEASTS
AND WHERE TO FIND THEM

FLOURISH & BLOTTS and OBSCURUS BOOKS
cordially invite you to the book launch of
NEWT SCAMANDER'S
FANTASTIC BEASTS
AND WHERE TO FIND THEM
Follow the writer in his worldwide quest for extraordinary creatures.
Saturday 19th of March - 7 o'clock
FLOURISH & BLOTTS
North Side · Diagon Alley · London
OBSCURUS

FACE VALUE

Pickett has long, sharp fingers on his hands, leaves for hair, tiny bulging eyes, and a slit for a mouth. The Bowtruckle's simple face did not require much animation beyond blinking eyes, but the digital artists did give him one definite facial reaction: He blows a raspberry at Newt when the Magizoologist asks him to smile.

NIFFLERS

Nifflers are mischievous, playful creatures that have a thick coat of black fur, beady eyes, and a snout-like nose. They are born with an instinctive penchant for shiny things and will go to great lengths to acquire pretty much anything that gleams, stashing their treasures in a seemingly bottomless pouch on their bellies.

GOTTA HAND IT TO YA

Platypuses, moles, and echidnas were referenced by the concept and digital artists for the Niffler's appearance. The Niffler's animators also made a point of watching videos that showed animals using their paws or hands as gathering tools, searching through dirt or mud for food. Among their best resources was a video of a honey badger ransacking a house, going through cupboards and even the refrigerator in its quest. They also looked at clips of "animal fails"—such as when a creature would miscalculate a jump and miss what they were after.

NUMEROUS NIFFLERS

Puppets of the Niffler were created for lighting and staging purposes, as well as acting as eyelines for the actors. Some contained a metal armature that could be repositioned as a scene progressed; others were made of silicone as "stunt" Nifflers. Hand puppets were created to be Niffler "stand-ins." One of the most important functions of the puppets was to provide a way for the actor and the creature to interact: their sizes, their movements, and even their characters. Pablo Grillo, who developed each creature's animation, would even act out the Niffler's mannerisms to show the filmmakers how it would react in a specific scene.

TICKLE ME NIFFLER

Actor Eddie Redmayne researched real-life animals for a better understanding of the magical creatures in *Fantastic Beasts and Where to Find Them*. For the Niffler, he observed a baby anteater, who would curl up into a little ball when nervous. To get the anteater to relax, the zoologist Redmayne worked with would tickle the anteater's belly. This led to the method Newt uses on the Niffler when he wants him to release the treasure he's acquired in a bank vault.

BABY NIFFLERS!

For *Fantastic Beasts: The Crimes of Grindelwald*, Newt attends to a family of baby Nifflers. Though these adorable scene stealers were created digitally, guinea pigs were referenced for the babies' size and fuzzy fur.

OCCAMY

Among the many creatures that escape from Newt's case in *Fantastic Beasts and Where to Find Them* is an Occamy chick, who's discovered hiding in one of New York's many department stores.

FISH AND FOWL

Occamies have a snakelike body covered in feathers, with the head of a bird of prey on top. When an Occamy is threatened, its skin turns iridescent, so animators looked at cuttlefish and chameleons for their changing skin patterns, as well as birds—specifically herons and hummingbirds—whose feathers can refract light, giving them a brilliant sheen.

CO-RA-NAP-WHAT?

An Occamy can grow or shrink to fit the size of its container—whether it's a multilevel department store loft or a tiny teapot. Author and screenwriter J.K. Rowling came up with a name to describe the Occamy's ability: choranaptyxic. Since Newt explains this power to Tina Goldstein, Eddie Redmayne worked with a dialogue coach to pronounce it. It's *cor-ra-nap-TISS-ick*, of course.

DEMIGUISE

The Demiguise is a rare creature, hunted for its silvery fur, which is used to make invisibility cloaks—for Demiguises are able to shift from visible to invisible. They also have the ability to see the future, so capturing an escaped Demiguise that knows what's about to happen and can disappear in response may get a bit tricky!

HAIR AND THERE

The shapes and fluid movements of primates and sloths were used for Demiguise references. Animators were challenged with developing the long, flowing hair that covers her entire body. And as the Demiguise literally goes on the run, her hair needed to wave in the wind. So, the digital artists used a software appropriately called Furtility!

ERUMPENT

The Erumpent is the largest creature Newt Scamander needs to return to his case in *Fantastic Beasts and Where to Find Them*. He finds her in Central Park in New York, but complicating her capture, the Erumpent is in heat! Newt must perform the Erumpent's mating dance with her in order to bring her back.

BIG IDEAS

Concept artist Rob Bliss looked at rhinoceroses, hippos, and bison for inspiration when designing the Erumpent. Though she's incredibly huge, the animators wanted to make her appear feminine but were worried about her seeming too "cartoony." Then, they discovered a video of a bison that had been brought into the house of a man in the Midwestern United States. Despite its size, the bison's cautious movements actually appeared dainty.

❖✦❖✦❖✦❖✦❖✦❖✦❖✦❖✦❖

WEIGHTY DECISIONS

In order to choreograph the actors and guide the animators through the Erumpent's scene, a wireframe structure that measured seventeen feet tall and twenty feet long was constructed out of carbon fiber. Four puppeteers operated the rig—two in front and two in back. While enacting the creature, the puppeteers, as well as the digital artists, needed to keep the laws of physics in mind, as its weight and size would influence its movements.

THE DANCE OF LOVE

Redmayne worked with a choreographer to create the mating dance of the Erumpent, which allows Newt to retrieve the creature without causing too much destruction. The actor remembers reading "Newt performs mating dance" in the script and thinking he'd never been more nervous about a scene! The mating dances of birds were studied, and then Redmayne created his own version, which was videotaped and shown to the filmmakers. The feedback? "Not seductive enough!" It took ten more versions before the final dance was chosen. A video of the selected dance was given to the digital team to animate, and then the puppeteers received a copy of that to rehearse the Erumpent's moves. After the scene was filmed, Redmayne was quite proud of being able to seduce an Erumpent.

THUNDERBIRD

The reason Newt Scamander travels to the United States is to return a trafficked Thunderbird to its native environment in Arizona. Thunderbirds have multiple wings that can draw in enough water vapor to create clouds that can then yield storms with lightning and rain. This creature becomes essential to saving New York City: It releases raindrops containing a potion that will Obliviate the memories of the No-Maj citizens as Aurors reconstruct roads and buildings ruined by an Obscurus.

TAKING WINGS

The design of the Thunderbird was inspired by the noble countenance of birds of prey; its head is shaped like a bald eagle's. The Occamy was originally intended to have multiple wings, as she was going to fly over the city in a scene, but this concept was reassigned when the Occamy ended up staying inside the department store. So, the idea was transferred to the Thunderbird, which enhanced its silhouette, differentiat-ing it from other bird-based creatures in the

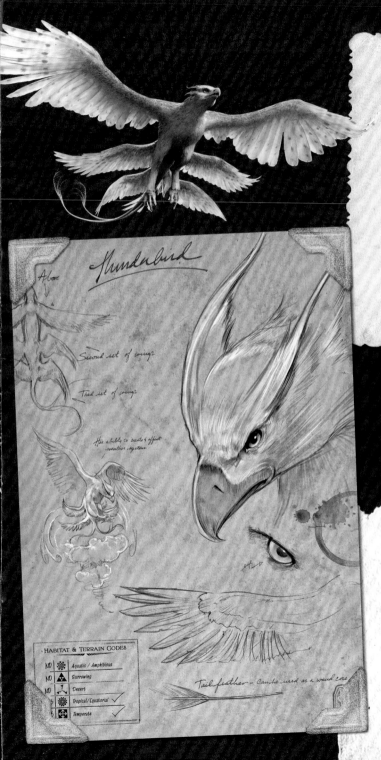

IN SYMPATHY WITH

A physical puppet of the Thunderbird's head was created for actor Eddie Redmayne to respond to when Newt visits the environments within his case. This wasn't just to provide an eyeline for the actor. Newt's relationship to the creature is so strong and so thoroughly exemplifies the affection and sympathy he has for the creatures he's protecting that the filmmakers felt it important to have at least a part of the Thunderbird for him to interact with.

THE CALM AFTER THE STORM

Taking a cue from its name and purpose, the Thunderbird's wings were animated to reflect the patterns of the clouds around it as it soars through the sky, and also to scatter beams of sunlight through them like a stained glass window. As the creature summons a storm while it flies, its feathers darken with the release of its energy.

INSIGHT
EDITIONS

PO Box 3088
San Rafael, CA 94912
www.insighteditions.com

Find us on Facebook: www.facebook.com/InsightEditions
Follow us on Twitter: @insighteditions

Library of Congress Cataloging-in-Publication Data available.

ISBN: 978-1-64722-412-7

Publisher: Raoul Goff
VP of Licensing and Partnerships: Vanessa Lopez
VP of Creative: Chrissy Kwasnik
VP of Manufacturing: Alix Nicholaeff
Editorial Director: Vicki Jaeger
Designer: Lola Villanueva
Senior Editor: Greg Solano
Editorial Assistant: Anna Wostenberg
Managing Editor: Lauren LePera
Senior Production Editor: Elaine Ou
Senior Production Manager: Greg Steffen
Senior Production Manager, Subsidiary Rights: Lina s Palma
Text: Jody Revenson

ROOTS of PEACE   REPLANTED PAPER

Insight Editions, in association with Roots of Peace, will plant two trees for each tree used in the manufacturing of this book. Roots of Peace is an internationally renowned humanitarian organization dedicated to eradicating land mines worldwide and converting war-torn lands into productive farms and wildlife habitats. Roots of Peace will plant two million fruit and nut trees in Afghanistan and provide farmers there with the skills and support necessary for sustainable land use.

Manufactured in China by Insight Editions

10 9 8 7 6 5 4 3 2